EUROPA  MILITARIA
SPECIAL No17

UNION TROOPS
of the
American Civil War

Jonathan Sutherland

THE CROWOOD PRESS

First published in 2005 by
The Crowood Press Ltd
Ramsbury, Marlborough
Wiltshire SN8 2HR

www.crowood.com

British Library Cataloguing-in-Publication Data
A catalogue record for this book is available from the British
Library.

ISBN 1 86126 769 X

Contents

Typeset by Jean Cussons Typesetting, Diss, Norfolk

Printed and bound in Singapore by Craft Print International

Introduction

AT the beginning of the American Civil War (1861–5), with the exception of the small regular army of the United States, the vast majority of soldiers went into battle dressed in their pre-war militia uniforms. The US Army, or Union Army, became the largest deployment of manpower that the United States had ever mustered; it would remain so until the USA entered the First World War in 1917.

In all, some 2.7 million men served in the Union Army over the period of the conflict. Up to 200,000 of these men, nearly 10 per cent, were African Americans who served in the guise of United States Colored Troops, infantry, artillery and cavalry. Just over 199,000 Union men deserted (many re-enlisting under an assumed name to claim a cash bounty). Over 183,000 died of diseases, around 95,000 were killed in action and 6,749 were posted missing in action.

In all, 1,666 infantry regiments were created (plus 306 independent infantry companies), 258 cavalry regiments (plus 170 independent cavalry companies) and 57 artillery regiments plus 22 heavy artillery companies and 232 light artillery batteries).

A Union soldier had better equipment than his Confederate opponent; there was also a more structured and prescribed organizational structure to the unit. A standard volunteer infantry regiment had between 640 and 820 enlisted men in ten companies; each company had three officers, thirteen non-commissioned officers and two musicians. A volunteer cavalry regiment consisted of four to six squadrons, each of two companies. Each company had three officers, fourteen non-commissioned officers, two buglers, two farriers (who doubled as veterinary surgeons), two blacksmiths, a saddler and around fifty-six privates. An artillery regiment had twelve batteries. Each battery consisted of four officers, up to sixteen non-commissioned officers, two musicians, up to six artificers (gun maintenance) and between 58 and 122 enlisted men.

The quality of the uniforms available in the early stages of the war left a great deal to be desired. The Washington government rushed to engage contractors to produce them and, as a result, the contractors took advantage of the situation, constructing most of the uniforms out of a processed material that was known as 'shoddy'. Trousers, in particular, fell to pieces when they got wet and it would be some time before the Union army instituted any form of quality control.

A standard infantryman, in addition to his basic trousers and jacket, would be given a cartridge box that held sixty rounds and was usually slung over his left shoulder. Around his belt were slung a percussion-cap box and his bayonet scabbard. Over his right shoulder went a waterproofed knapsack carrying his rations and a tin water bottle covered in wool. He was also issued with a blanket or an overcoat, which he would also keep in his knapsack; some of the men rolled these up in an oilcloth that was slung on the left shoulder, extending down to the right hip. Initially, at least, the men were given single-shot percussion-lock muskets. Cavalry were similarly equipped, except that they were given a sabre, a pistol and a carbine. At this stage artillerymen were only issued with swords.

By 1862 Washington had decreed that the men should only carry a single blanket, a pair of shirts, two pairs of undergarments, two pairs of socks, a jacket or a blouse, a pair of trousers, a hat or a cap, a greatcoat and a pair of black brogan shoes.

In the early stages of the war officers differed little from the enlisted men. They would be armed with a pistol and a sabre and, aside from having their rank insignia on their uniforms, there would be little to distinguish them from the rank and file.

The Union Army was a very different fighting force to the Confederates. Many of the men were drawn from large urban areas, or at least small towns. The pay was adequate but not spectacular; initially it was $13 per month, but this rose to $16 in May 1864. At the same time an unskilled labourer could expect to earn $20 per month.

Rations were adequate but uninspiring: salt beef and hard bread made up the bulk of the food issued to the troops. Later, desiccated vegetables were supplied, which when mixed with water produced a soup.

After the first battle of Bull Run (Manassas) in July 1861, the hope that this single battle would decide the outcome of the war was dashed. At Bull Run, New York National Guard regiments (part of the Union Army) formed up in grey uniforms while many Confederate units still wore blue. However, after this first major engagement of the war Washington, like the Confederacy, began to lay down dress regulations. The Union's regulations were far more formal and rigorously applied than those of the south. As the quality issues were addressed, not only were the northern troops far better clothed and equipped, but their possessions became much coveted by their less-fortunate Confederate opponents.

With the exception of specific units such as sharpshooter regiments that wore green, and Zouave regiments that wore predominantly dark blue uniforms and their distinctive red fez and ballooned trousers, the Union soldiers wore strikingly similar uniforms to one another, distinguishable only by the piping that denoted branch of service. The Union blue ultimately became the uniform of the United States Armed Forces for the next fifty years.

Unlike the more flamboyant Confederate regiments, the Union Army could hardly be described as being dressy. Many of the men were issued with dark-blue frock coats and a fatigue blouse and cap. The dress hats were almost universally despised and the most popular cap, variously known as a forage or fatigue cap, or kepi, was worn by in excess of three quarters of all Union troops.

This book and its companion, *Confederate Troops of the American Civil War*, depict British-based re-enactors of the American Civil War Society, which is the largest American Civil War re-enactment group outside the USA. They currently have nearly 1,000 regular re-enactors representing, on the Union side, units including 1st US Sharpshooters, 2nd Wisconsin, 8th Ohio, 19th Indiana, 54th Michigan, 69th New York, 118th Pennsylvania, 2nd US Artillery and 4th Michigan Cavalry. Their website can be found at www.acws.co.uk or ACWS, PO Box 52, Brighouse, West Yorkshire, HD6 1JQ.

Union Infantry Officers

UNION infantry officers were issued with dark-blue frock coats that extended to around two thirds of the way between the waist and the knee. They had a standing collar with pockets in the skirt folds, and three buttons on each cuff. A company-grade officer would have a row of nine buttons down the front, while other, more senior, field officers would have two rows of seven buttons. The officers were issued with gilt epaulettes, usually only worn for parades and special occasions. As they were infantry officers, the coloured disc on their epaulettes was sky blue. A colonel would have a silver eagle on his epaulette strap, a lieutenant colonel a silver leaf, a captain would have two silver bars and a first lieutenant a single bar. In the field, however, the officers would wear transverse shoulder straps with the same insignia as on the epaulette, but this time in gold embroidery.

Officers wore blue, white or buff waistcoats. In practice the blue colours were more dominant, and these were made with standing collars and four slashed pockets. Many regimental officers also wore a crimson silk-net sash passed twice around the waist and tied at the left hip, secured by their belt; these were rarely worn in the field, however, as they drew enemy fire. Just like their Confederate counterparts, Union officers, although rather more flamboyant in dress than their enlisted men, did try to disguise themselves to an extent in order to avoid being picked off by the enemy.

(Opposite) This regimental captain is wearing a frock coat with a single row of nine buttons. Around his waist is a crimson sash, tied at the left hip; on parade the wearing of the sash would denote the officer of the day. He carries an M1850 officer's sword, which has a slightly curved blade that is just over an inch (2.5cm) wide at the hilt. The scabbard provided was of black leather and iron. The officer wears a brass Union eagle belt-buckle and is probably issued with a Colt six-shot, single-action revolver, with a walnut grip and a brass trigger guard. He wears the folding Union officers' slouch hat, with a brass hunting-horn device designating that he is an infantry officer. The wearing of this device was strictly enforced in the Eastern Theatre, but not so much in the Western Theatre.

(Below) According to the regulations all officers were meant to wear a frock coat of dark-blue cloth, the skirt to extend from two thirds to three fourths of the distance from the top of the hip to the bend of the knee. The coat was to be single-breasted for captains and lieutenants, and double-breasted for all other officer ranks. They were to wear an ornament on the front of their hats: this was a gold-embroidered bugle on black velvet ground, with the number of the regiment in silver within the bend. Commissioned officers could also wear forage caps of the same pattern as enlisted men, with the distinctive ornament of the corps and regiment in front. They could also wear a black cravat, with the tie to be visible at the opening of the collar.

(**Opposite**) This officer has opted to wear the pattern 1858 forage or fatigue cap. He still wears his frock coat and appears to be carrying a Model 1860 sabre, still in its protective scabbard, over his shoulder. The straps for his equipment, including that of his water bottle, can clearly be seen crossing his chest. He appears to be wearing a white stand-up collar shirt under his frock coat. The army purchased 374,000 revolvers for its officers and mounted men; the navy .36-calibre revolver was the most popular and many of the officers bought their own weapons as they considered them to be easier to handle and a much more practical size than the issue revolvers.

(**Below**) Officers were to wear waist belts not less than 1½in (3.8cm) nor more than 2in (5cm) wide, to be worn over the sash. The sword was to be suspended from it by slings of the same material as the belt, with a hook attached to the belt allowing the sword to be hung. The sword-belt plate was gilt, rectangular, 2in (5cm) wide with a raised bright rim and a silver wreath of laurel encircling the 'Arms of the United States', the eagle and shield. It was to have a scroll, edge of cloud and bright rays of sunlight. The motto, *E Pluribus Unum*, in silver letters, upon the scroll; stars also of silver; according to pattern. The sword and sword-belt were to be worn on all occasions of duty, without exception.

(Left) Officers were required to purchase their own uniforms while enlisted men were issued uniforms from the Quartermaster. The Quartermaster required that enlisted men's clothing and insignia conform to army regulations and by and large they did conform. Officers had a little more discretion, but the military tailors and military outfitters who supplied the uniform items were aware of the requirements of the regulations. In the regulations, the sword-belt is described in detail, but the oval US plate is not. Corps badges were introduced in 1862 and these do not appear in the regulations. They were adopted by General Orders and then issued by the respective commands in the army.

(Above) This Union infantry officer wears a standard jacket with shoulder boards, denoting that he is an infantry officer. This officer sports the style of facial hair that was popular during the American Civil War. The extended sideboards were made popular by Ambrose Burnside, hence the term 'sideburns'. Burnside was an 1847 West Point graduate and led a regiment at the First Bull Run (Manassas) in 1861. He had a meteoric rise to fame, replacing George McClelland as the Commander of the Army of the Potomac after Antietam in September 1862.

Union Flags and Drummers

DURING the Civil War, as far as Union troops were concerned, there were at least eight different types of banner carried by a wide variety of different units. Traditionally, red stood for valour, white for purity and blue for vigilance, perseverance and justice. Each infantry regiment carried a national or state colour and a regimental flag. The flag signified their allegiance to the Union and the regimental colour identified them as troops from a particular state.

The US Army regulations of 1861 revised the construction of the Union flag. It was to have thirteen horizontal stripes of equal breadth, alternating red and white and beginning with red. The Union itself was represented by a number of white stars in the upper left corner, equal to the number of states in the Union (nineteen). The stars were on a blue field, approximately one third of the length of the flag and extending to the lower edge of the fourth red stripe from the top.

Many of the volunteer regiments began the war with their own regimental bands of varying sizes. These men would have been a mixture of drummers, fifers and buglers; in some cases they carried the full range of brass instruments. Ultimately, while buglers and drummers remained integral parts of the regiments, regimental bands were scaled down as they were considered to be wasteful of manpower. Henceforth regiments were permitted to retain their buglers and drummers in limited numbers, but true bands were only attached in some cases at brigade, and in most cases at divisional, level.

(Right) This standard-bearer carries a national colour – the regimental designation would be embroidered in silver on the middle red stripe. It essentially followed the same regulations as the revised instructions for the national flag, which required that the flag clearly indicate the regiment's name and number. The flags were approximately 6ft × 6ft 6in (1.8 × 2m), the fringe was yellow and the cords of the tassels were a mixture of red and yellow silk. Generally the flag's pole was 9ft 10in (3m) long, including the spear and ferrule. The white stars were embroidered, since originally the flags had been painted and the silver and gold tarnished very quickly. In January 1862 the Federal Government took over the responsibility for supplying all units with their flags. The US Quartermaster's Department established depots in Philadelphia, New York and Cincinnati to deal with the huge demand as literally hundreds of regiments were raised.

(**Left**) A regimental flag is seen here, which has a blue field with the coat of arms of the USA embroidered in silk at the centre; the regimental designation is included on a scroll underneath. Again the flag is 6ft × 6ft 6in (1.8 × 2m), producing a narrow, rectangular flag. The fringe was yellow and the cords were blue and white silk. The pole, including the spear and ferrule, was 9ft 10in (3m). Earlier Union Civil War flags did not have the US coat of arms but instead featured the state's coat of arms. It was only after the Federal government began supplying flags to all regiments that gradually, largely due to wear and tear, flags featuring the US coat of arms replaced the state flags.

(Right) This Stars and Stripes flag is identical to the standard garrison flag. The garrison flags, constructed and based on the revised 1861 regulations, were far larger at 20ft high and 36ft in length (6 × 11m); in all other respects they were identical to the flags carried by the individual regiments. This flag is seen beside a parade of infantrymen in camp. Camp colours were used to mark the borders of the military camp. They were often made of bunting, effectively a woven wool fabric; infantrymen used white camp colours and sometimes the bunting would be carried into battle to assist the regiments in lining up. The camp colours were usually mounted on an 8ft (2.4m) pole and were about 18ft (5.5m) square. Post-January 1862 they were imprinted with the New York depot Stars and Stripes.

(Opposite) Here we can clearly see the stars on the Stars and Stripes regimental flag. In all likelihood this was a representation of the Union Iron Brigade, a mix of troops from Michigan, Indiana and Wisconsin. On the battlefield, in addition to the regimental flags, the Union adopted a new system in 1863: a swallowtail flag would mark a corps headquarters, a rectangular one a division headquarters and a triangular flag a brigade headquarters. Each division could be identified as it had a unique mix of the corps badge and background colour – for example, a blue badge on a white field would designate the 3rd division of a corps. The colour patterns continued down to the brigades of each of the divisions.

(Right) This Union bugler carries an all-brass instrument. Note the white silk tassels attached to the bugle. The bugler would play an important role, both in camp and on the battlefield. In combat, due to the noise and smoke, it was difficult for officers and NCOs to pass on orders and instructions to the men, so simple bugle calls were rehearsed to which the men would be able to respond, such as changing formation, falling back or charging.

(Below) Youngsters, such as these drummer boys, were drawn to the Union Army in large numbers. They were kitted out with specially made or altered uniforms to fit them, and dressed in every way as a standard infantryman. The drums would bear the Union coat of arms, and state and regimental decoration. The most famous drummer boy of the Civil War was Johnny Lincoln Clem, who signed up with the 22nd Michigan at the age of nine. He was paid $13 a month by the officers of the regiment. He was present at the battles of Shiloh and Chickamauga, and at the latter he killed a Confederate officer who had ordered him to surrender. Clem was wounded twice during the war and eventually joined the regular army in 1871; he retired in 1916, by which time he had attained the rank of major general.

(**Right**) Many of the bugles were French Model 1845 infantry bugles. In this case the bugler has red silk tassels attached to the instrument. He wears a mid-blue Union overcoat with cape – note the extensive cuff. Soldiers' lives were controlled by the sound of the bugle. The US Army had since 1835 used the 'tattoo', which was a camp order to extinguish lights. Eventually the still-used taps would replace this, which is generally credited to Brigadier General Daniel Butterfield, who came up with the idea in July 1862 at Harrison's Landing, Virginia.

Union Infantry Enlisted Men

AS war loomed in 1861 literally thousands of men from northern cities, towns and villages flocked to join the Union Army. Many of them marched to war with only a rudimentary understanding of their weapons and virtually no knowledge of drill. Volunteers received a cash bonus and although the pay did not in any way compare to even the income of an unskilled labourer, what motivated the men to volunteer was the threat of being conscripted and missing out on the cash bonus.

Most of the first volunteers enlisted for ninety days, some for a year – it was generally expected that the war would be concluded by the summer of 1861. The northern states were expected to fulfil enlistment quotas and, as a result, many of the states offered large enlistment bounties or bonuses to those who initially enlisted and subsequently re-enlisted after their first tour of duty. Around half of the men had been farmers, though records indicate that the Union Army enlisted men from 300 different occupations. Initially the bulk of the men were white, Protestant and unmarried. The vast majority were aged between eighteen and twenty-nine, although there were innumerable sixteen- and seventeen-year-olds who passed themselves off as eighteen. The youngest soldier from the north was Edward Black, who joined the 21st Indiana as a musician at the age of nine years.

Among the hundreds of thousands of men who would serve in the Union Army were upward of 200,000 African American troops, authorization for their service being granted in January 1863, several months after Lincoln's Emancipation Proclamation.

At the time of the Confederate surrenders during April and May 1865, the Union Army had 1,034,000 men in uniform, serving from the Atlantic to the Pacific Ocean and from the Gulf of Mexico to the Ohio River. The many thousands of blue-clad Union soldiers had prevailed and by November 1865, 800,000 of the men had been mustered out, at a cost of $270m in back pay and promised bounty payments for having served in the Union's armed forces. By February 1866 the new United States Army had shrunk to 80,000 men.

(**Below**) According to Army Regulations dated 1861, the infantry were instructed to wear buttons 'gilt, convex; device, a spread eagle with the letter I, for Infantry, large size, seven-eighths of an inch in exterior diameter; small size, one-half inch'. The uniform coat specified for all enlisted infantrymen was a single-breasted frock coat of dark-blue cloth, made without plaits, with a skirt extending half the distance from the top of the hip to the bend of the knee. It was fastened by nine buttons, placed at equal distances. The stand-up collar was to rise no higher than to permit the chin to turn freely over it, to hook in front at the bottom and then to slope up and backward at an angle of thirty degrees on each side. The cuffs were pointed according to pattern, and secured by two small buttons at the under seam. The collar and cuffs were edged with a cord or welt of cloth in sky blue.

(**Opposite**) This picture represents the archetypal Union infantryman. He wears a pattern 1858 forage, fatigue or kepi-style cap. Theoretically, peacetime infantrymen, and certainly some early units in the Civil War, were issued with hats for dress occasions. In practice, however, for economic and practical reasons the Union infantryman usually only received the kepi. In fact, in 1861 the command of the Army of the Potomac issued a string of orders that non-issue headgear was to be either confiscated or burned. From at least September 1864 officers were threatened with arrest if they allowed their men to wear anything other than the kepi.

(**Right**) Sniping, or 'sharpshooting', was a much-used psychological weapon during the Civil War. Aside from the well-documented Berdan's Sharpshooters, many other Union marksmen saw action. A formal muster of sharpshooters was not practicable, but in correspondence between the Governor of Rhode Island, William Sprague, and the Union Secretary of War, Edwin Stanton, the notion was that the men would be best deployed in units no larger than a company, which would be attached to regiments for special deployment.

The men were armed with a variety of weapons including Sharp's rifles, Whitworth rifles and sporting arms as well as custom-made and privately owned target weapons. Marksmen were used at Yorktown, Gettysburg, Vicksburg, Chattanooga, Atlanta, Spotsylvania, the Wilderness and Petersburg. They were much valued in any form of protracted battle and contributed to the high death toll of officers and non-commissioned officers.

(**Below**) Enlisted infantrymen received both the frock coat, worn by the man on the left, and the fatigue blouse, as worn by the two other infantrymen in this picture. Practicalities meant that quartermasters often found it impossible to supply the men with both jackets. During the summer months the men habitually wore their fatigue blouses and many hundreds of them threw away extraneous clothing to reduce the amount they had to carry. Orders were issued from 1863 that each spring the men would put their additional gear into storage rather than jettison it on the march. The regiment itself decided when and where the men would wear their frock coats or fatigue blouses, and sometimes this decision would be left to the company officer.

(**Opposite**) Although the majority of the men chose to wear the more comfortable fatigue blouse, some men decided to reserve their frock coats for going into battle. This infantryman wears his unadorned fatigue blouse, standard-issue kepi, light-blue trousers and black brogue shoes. He has tucked his trousers into his socks, as he has not been issued with gaiters. His blanket or bedroll is securely housed in a waterproof roll and has been slung over his back. The infantryman appears to be carrying a British 1853-pattern Enfield rifle musket, a weapon that was imported in enormous numbers.

(**Right**) The Union Army commissioned the construction of over 41,500 forage caps (also known as fatigue caps or kepis – the caps were made in the French kepi style); in addition they purchased 4.7 million between mid-May 1861 and October 1865. The kepi was made of dark wool, with a pasteboard circular sheet forming the top surface. It was taller at the rear than at the front so that the crown inclined forwards. It was lined with polished cotton in black or brown and usually had a maker's label pasted onto the inside. The peak was made of black, glazed leather. In this case the peak slopes down slightly over the wearer's eyes, although other peaks were horizontal. Two brass buttons secured the leather chinstrap. The brass buckle is purely decorative. The chinstrap was adjustable so that it could be worn around the peak or around the chin.

(**Opposite top**) Generally dress hats were unpopular, but despite this the men of the Army of the Potomac's Iron Brigade, such as the bearded infantryman in this picture, habitually wore their dress hats. Although in this example the infantryman has the bugle horn, many of the men wore no adornments on their hats at all. The infantryman wears a nine-buttoned frock coat with two small buttons on each cuff. He lacks brass shoulder scales. In excess of 1.8 million dress coats were purchased between May 1861 and June 1865. Normally the enlisted soldier's frock coat had branch of service colours around the collar and the cuff. This infantryman wears a circular brass plate featuring an eagle holding three arrows in one of his talons. Similar circular brass plates would be found on a non-commissioned officer's sword-belt – in this case it is on his cartridge-box cross belt.

(**Opposite below**) The majority of these men wear a frock coat and the black felt hat. These hats were made to have a 6¼in (15.9cm) crown and a 3¼in (8.3cm) brim, though many of the hats were actually smaller than this. The brim was hooked up on the left side, which often concealed a brass or embroidered eagle badge. A single ostrich feather was worn on the opposite side of the hat to the brim in the case of enlisted men: company-grade officers wore two feathers and field officers, three. The hats in this example are decorated with hat cords made of worsted; the tassels usually extended to around 2in (5cm) and were often worn on the side of the hat opposite the feather. The infantryman in the centre has a brass Jäger or bugle horn badge. Above this decoration is his company letter, in this case an A.

(**Above**) This infantry corporal wears a frock coat and standard kepi. Theoretically the men were also issued with a black oilcloth cap cover. Around 675,000 of these were purchased; many of the cap covers did not fit and the men resorted to making their own from rubber blankets. This corporal is fully accoutred with a black leather knapsack, wool-covered water bottle and bayonet scabbard. Many of the men embellished their kepis with company letters and officers added their corps or regimental insignia. The vast majority of the men, over 60 per cent in fact, wore no decoration on their kepis of any type. Less than 20 per cent wore their brass regimental numbers or branch of service, while fewer than 20 per cent wore their cloth corps badges.

(**Left**) The two men in the rear line of this column wear (left) a frock coat and (right) a sack coat. The sack coat was made of dark-blue flannel. It reached to approximately halfway down the thigh and was fastened with four coat buttons at the front. Washington purchased in excess of 3.6 million lined sack coats, which were usually distributed to recruits; 1.8 million unlined sack coats were also produced. The lining was of a coarse, grey flannel and the coats were invariably worn with the collars straight up and fastened with hooks and eyes. In the majority of photographs of the Army of the Potomac, upwards of 46 per cent of the men wore fatigue coats of this description, the others wearing a mixture of fatigue blouses and frock coats.

(Below) According to 1855 regulations, the infantryman's buttons were to be gilt, convex and have a spread-eagle design with the letter 'I'. They were just short of an inch (2.5cm) in diameter in the large size and half this size for smaller buttons. This veteran infantryman has a blue cravat: it is of unofficial design, as the army purchased three quarters of a million black leather stocks during the war, few of which were ever worn. This infantryman's waist belt has an oval-shaped, stamped brass plate. It was backed with lead and on the front had simple 'US' letters embellished on it. Officers and non-commissioned officers would have worn a brass plate with an applied silver wreath, which was an ornate design featuring the spread-eagle with a chevron-type shield covering its body.

(Right) This sergeant has three chevrons on his sleeve, just above the elbow. Sergeant majors had three bars and arcs, quartermaster sergeants had three bars and a straight tie, first sergeants had three bars and a lozenge, and a corporal would have two bars; pioneers would be marked with crossed hatchets. On his back this infantryman has a standard-issue knapsack of black-painted cotton. It was approximately $12\frac{1}{2} \times 3 \times 13$in ($32 \times 8 \times 33$cm). It has a 5in (13cm) flap with a single leather strap. The infantryman would carry a white cotton bag for his food inside, which was held in place by three tin buttons.

(Left) This infantry private is in standard kit, with dyed sky-blue trousers, which tended to have a greenish hue after several washes. The army purchased over 6 million pairs of these trousers during the war. They had five tin fly buttons and four buttons around the waist for the attachment of braces, which were not actually standard issue. Most of the trousers had a slit in the rear, with two holes. The soldier would put twine or rawhide into the two holes provided to adjust the size of the waist. The pockets were straight cut, but in some cases they had flaps. Sometimes the trousers were made with a watch pocket on the right waistband.

(Opposite) This first sergeant has his three bars and lozenge to designate his rank. On his back he has the standard-issue knapsack; this was actually two bags attached at the top and strapped together at the bottom. It was slung over the shoulders, held in place by two 2in-wide (5cm) shoulder straps and designed to hook up to the front of the 1855 rifleman's belt. In practice, however, these belts were in short supply and it was more usual for the men to hook the straps across the chest and onto the opposite shoulder strap, and sometimes under the waist belt. Most of the knapsacks were marked with the regimental number, about 1.5in (4cm) in height. The army acquired approximately 3.5 million of these knapsacks between 1861 and 1866.

(Left) This infantryman represents an enlisted man from the 20th Maine, part of V Corps, as distinguished by the red Maltese cross. He has his company letter, F, placed over the corps badge on his kepi. The Union Army adopted corps badges from March 1863: I Corps had a circle; II Corps a stalked shamrock; III Corps a diamond or lozenge; IV Corps an equilateral triangle; VI Corps a Greek cross; VII Corps a crescent encircling a star; VIII a six-pointed star; IX Corps a shield with a figure 9; X Corps a four-sided fort; XI Corps a crescent; XII a star; XIV Corps an acorn; XV Corps a cartridge box; XVI Corps a circle with four balls; XVII Corps an arrow; XVIII Corps a cross; XIX Corps a four-pointed star; XX Corps a star; XXII Corps a cinquefoil; XXIII Corps a shield; XXIV Corps a heart; and XXV Corps a square. Neither XIII Corps nor XXI Corps adopted a badge.

(Opposite) These two infantrymen display their cartridge boxes, which were made of heavy black leather. A brass stud kept the flap closed and there were two vertical loops at the back, allowing the cartridge box to be worn on the waist belt, and two horizontal loops so that it could alternatively be worn on the shoulder belt. Universally, they had an oval, stamped, brass plate with 'US' imprinted on it. Later in the war this brass plate was replaced by an oval border and 'US' stamped into the leather. The box could carry two tins, each of which could hold a bundle of ten cartridges. Additional loose cartridges could be housed in the upper part of the box.

(**Below**) This infantry column displays a variety of footwear. The standard-issue boot or shoe was an ankle-high laced boot. It had the rough side of the leather outside and the soles could either be pegged or sewn; the Union Army bought 1.5 million sewn shoes and just over 1 million pegged-sole shoes. Theoretically the infantryman was to receive four pairs a year, but in practice six days of marching would see a pair of shoes in a deplorable state. The brogan-style shoe, as they were known, were often provided with extremely thin soles. Many of the men bought lightweight white canvas and brown leather sporting shoes, and in some cases these types of shoes were actually issued to the men.

(**Opposite below**) Two of the men in this picture are wearing the Union blue overcoat. The enlisted man was issued with a sky-blue wool coat with a standing collar and a single row of five buttons. They also had an elbow-length cape that was fastened with six buttons. During the war the Union Army purchased 2.8 million of these overcoats and, in its desperation to ensure that the men did not suffer during the winter months, other colours of overcoats were issued, including black, brown and dark blue. The officer on the far right of the picture wears an enlisted man's overcoat. Officers were allowed to do this by regulation in order to make themselves less visible as the commissioned officer's overcoat was dark blue with black silk across the chest.

(**Opposite top**) This unit of Union infantry accompanied by a Berdan sharpshooter is ready to move off from camp. Again a variety of shoes and a single instance of the wearing of gaiters can be seen. The gaiters were not a regulation part of the uniform, although many regiments drew supplies of these and wore them. It had been the army's intention that gaiters would be worn as early as 1860. Some regiments insisted that all of their men wore the white gaiters around their ankles, such as the 7th Pennsylvania Reserves and the 110th Pennsylvania Infantry. In most instances the gaiters were distributed to Zouave regiments rather than regular infantry units. They were made of heavy white linen and were approximately 10.5in (27cm) high and were kept in place by six tin buttons and a 1.5in (4cm) black leather strap that passed under the instep and was secured by a button.

(Opposite) This Union sergeant, marching alongside the colour party in an infantry column, is undoubtedly a first sergeant, as he has a red worsted sash in crimson with bullion fringe ends. Between 1861 and 1865 the Union Army purchased 25,717 of these sashes. They were supposed to be worn for most duties, but the officers and non-commissioned officers were not expected to wear them in the field. It was standard practice for the men to wear these sashes around their waist on normal occasions, but if they were given special duties for the day they would wear the sash across their right shoulder to their left hip.

(Right) This stand of basic infantry equipment includes muskets, waist belt, cartridge- and cap boxes, tin cup and wool-covered canteen. Also visible is the bayonet scabbard. The army issued steel socket bayonets for the Enfield and Springfield rifle muskets. They were 18in (44cm) long with triangular-section blades and were designed in such a way to allow them to be mounted onto the sight stud on the musket barrel. The scabbard was approximately 19.5in (50cm) long, with a brass end. The water bottle or canteen was made of tin with a pewter mouthpiece; it usually had three tin loops through which a cotton strap was threaded. Many of the canteens had cork stoppers with a tin cap on top, which was held in place with an iron pin.

(Left) In theory at least the standard infantry musket was the M1842 smoothbore. Many M1855 rifled muskets were produced, but the M1861 became the standard infantry musket. It was produced by twenty-two different manufacturers in the USA, as well as being provided by exporters from Belgium and Germany. Over 670,000 were made. The most popular foreign-made musket was the British Enfield: this became the second most important infantry musket in the Union Army, which purchased 428,292 of them during the war years. Large numbers of Austrian Lorenz rifled muskets were also imported, as were Prussian, Belgian and French muskets.

(Opposite) This first sergeant has a dark blue stripe down the leg of his trousers. Around half of non-commissioned officers adopted this style in line with the 1861 regulations. Officially, non-commissioned officers and enlisted men were supposed to have a branch-of-service colour stripe down their trousers; in this case the stripe is approximately 1.5in (4cm) wide. Regulation changes in 1861 changed the colour from dark blue to sky blue for officers, but retained the dark-blue stripe for non-commissioned officers.

(Left) This sergeant major has a sky-blue faced frock coat, sash around the waist, visible bayonet scabbard and straps across his chest for his water bottle and cartridge box. Clearly visible is his waistcoat; these were issued to officers, non-commissioned officers and enlisted men alike. Officers could wear buff, white or blue waistcoats, but the most common were the dark and sky-blue variants. The majority of them had a row of small brass buttons down the front and a belt and buckle on the rear for size adjustment. Photographs taken of men in the Army of the Potomac during the war indicate that at least 20 per cent of the men wore waistcoats. They were particularly prized as an additional layer of clothing during inclement weather.

(Opposite) These infantrymen, on a route march, display the full range of equipment carried by an infantryman in the field, including blankets. The US Army purchased nearly 6 million blankets in grey-brown wool with 'US' stitched in black letters in the centre. They also purchased 1.8 million rubber-coated blankets and 1.6 million ponchos. The main difference between the rubber-coated blankets and the ponchos was that the ponchos had a slit so that they could be worn over the head as a rain cape, while the blankets were simply that – blankets. They were both around 60in wide by 71in long (150 × 180cm) and they were fitted with brass eyelets so that they could be used as additional waterproofing for the men's tents.

(Right) These fully accoutred infantrymen on parade in camp wear the familiar kepi, while some have adopted the dress hat. The Stars and Stripes regimental flag and the Union blue flag are clearly visible. Some of the men have gaiters, while others have socks. The army purchased over 20 million grey or tan woollen socks. For the most part the socks were useless after 48 hours of wear: they were shoddily made and when they split at the foot the men often put on a second pair and relegated the original pair to serve as improvised gaiters, held up with string. There seems to have been little attempt made to try to mend the socks, and the men preferred to acquire their own from home.

(Left) This injured infantryman belongs to II Corps. His kepi is unadorned, other than his corps insignia. He appears to be wearing a sack coat over which are his knapsack straps, cartridge-belt strap and a cotton strap securing his canteen. He carries his musket reversed, a tactic often used by the infantry to prevent rainwater or debris falling down the barrel. Musket fouling was a constant problem and after a few shots the barrels would often contain debris from previous rounds that could make the musket fire prematurely, or refuse to fire at all.

(Right) In September 1861 the Union Army ordered 10,000 sets of French-style uniforms, which consisted of short jackets with piped detail, baggy trousers, gaiters and fez hats with long tassels. Many of the uniforms were dark-blue trimmed with red tape, and red trousers and fez. These became known as the Zouave dress and were distributed to several regiments from Pennsylvania and New York; other regiments soon adopted this style of clothing. Essentially they were chasseur uniforms, very much in the French style. Some regiments retained the fez while others adopted turbans. Zouave-dressed infantry were present at virtually every major battle of the war.

(Opposite) At the command 'load' the infantryman stood his rifle between his feet. He then reached into his cartridge box for a cartridge and placed the paper-wrapped powder and bullet between his teeth and tore the paper. He then poured the powder and ball into the muzzle of his rifle, drew his rammer and drove the ball down the bore so that it sat on the powder charge. After replacing the rammer he primed his musket by pulling the hammer to the half-cocked position and then reaching into his cap box for a cap, which he then placed on the nipple. He then shouldered his weapon, assumed the firing position and used his thumb to pull the hammer to full cock. He then aimed, sighting the weapon using the V notch and the sight at the end of the muzzle: he would then be ready to deliver an aimed shot.

United States Colored Troops

UPWARDS of 200,000 African American freemen and runaway slaves volunteered to join the Union Army. At first they were not wanted and were simply used as labourers to free up white soldiers. Ultimately, after the Emancipation Proclamation, a host of African-American regiments with white officers and mostly white non-commissioned officers was established in the northern states. Among the most famous was the 54th Massachusetts, led by Colonel Robert Gould Shaw, which was involved in innumerable actions in the Carolinas. The USCT or United States Colored Troops, as they became known, provided regular infantry regiments, cavalry and artillery. Some of the early regiments were even provided with Zouave-type uniforms.

African American soldiers were fittingly present at Lee's surrender at Appomattox, and had taken part in the vicious fighting around Petersburg and Richmond in the closing months of the war in 1865.

(Below) The vast majority of the US colored infantry regiments wore the regulation sky-blue trousers and dark-blue jackets. The famous 54th Massachusetts was mustered into service in May 1863. After seeing service on James Island in the July and Secessionville later in the month, the unit moved to Morris Island. The Union Army was attempting to take Charleston, but blocking its path was Fort Wagner. Colonel Robert Gould Shaw volunteered his regiment to lead the attack on the fort; under tremendous fire, the men broke through the defences and burst into the fort, with huge casualties. Shaw was killed at the top of the parapet and the assault was defeated.

(Right) These Union colored infantry are identically equipped to standard regular infantrymen. They display the short jacket and the figure in the foreground wears a sack coat. Their uniforms are relatively plain. The 1st South Carolina Volunteer Infantry wore frock coats with red trousers: this was one of the first African-American units to be formed and had its first taste of action along the coast of Georgia and Florida in November 1862, just a month after the Emancipation Proclamation. In February 1864 the regiment was re-designated as the 33rd US Colored Infantry. Their red trousers were then replaced with the standard blue issue ones.

Iron and Irish Brigades

THE Iron Brigade was also known as the Wisconsin Black Hat Brigade, although the brigade comprised three regiments of Wisconsin and one from Indiana. Later a Michigan regiment was added to replace losses. The Iron Brigade was also sometimes known as Rufus King's Brigade and had a distinctive style of uniform.

Around 150,000 Irishmen flocked to the Union cause. At least twenty regiments, including Brigadier General Meagher's Irish Brigade, were composed almost entirely of men from Ireland. The Irish Brigade itself consisted of the 9th, 63rd and 88th New York Infantry Regiments.

(**Left**) Their Hardee hats pinned up on one side, dark-blue frock coats and light-blue trousers typified the Iron Brigade. Invariably they wore the brass bugle on their hats, a sky-blue cord with tassels, and black ostrich feathers. To all other intents and purposes they were accoutred in exactly the same way as the regular infantrymen. Many of the men in the Iron Brigade were Irishmen and other immigrants, such as Germans. They suffered 33 per cent losses at the second battle of Bull Run (Manassas) in 1862. During the whole second Bull Run campaign 60 per cent of their numbers were lost.

(Right) This infantryman represents a sergeant of the 19th Indiana Regiment, which was a part of the Iron Brigade. The hat tended not to be folded, as was the practice in other regiments, but it would have an eagle shield standard on the right-hand side. The black plume was standard, as was the sky-blue infantry worsted hat cord. The brass Jäger horn and company affiliation would also be included on the hat, as would a red I Corps felt disc. The men wore the US infantry frock or sack coat, although the majority preferred the frock coat.

(Below) The three Wisconsin regiments initially went to war in grey uniforms and grey hats with a whalebone stiffener, making the hat stand up like a shako. However, at the first battle of Bull Run, in July 1861, the 69th New York fired on the 2nd Wisconsin in error. Consequently, in the late summer of 1861 the blue frock or sack coat, light-blue kersey trousers and the original-style hat were adopted, but in October of the same year Hardee hats and frock coats were issued. The men also adopted slightly darker-blue trousers initially, but by early 1863 they had reverted to the standard sky-blue trousers. By May 1862 the entire brigade had been kitted out with Hardee hats, frock coats and gaiters. The men were also issued with white gloves.

(**Opposite**) This Iron Brigade corporal clearly displays his white gaiters over the tops of his shoes and extending up to his calf. By the spring of 1863 the corps badge began appearing on the hats, and while the 19th Indiana and 6th Wisconsin retained their frock coats, in the 2nd and the 7th Wisconsin the sack coat became the more generally worn garment. Many of the men chose knapsacks rather than blanket rolls to carry their belongings; these were also useful in saving the men from injury from shell fragments.

(**Right**) The 69th New York wore an eight-button jacket. At Antietam the regiment piled up their knapsacks prior to their assault and several of the men pulled off their shoes and marched into battle barefoot. They drove the Confederates, under General D.H. Hill, out of their positions, at the cost of 113 killed and 422 wounded.

(**Below**) By late 1862 the Iron Brigade infantry had a mixture of frock and sack coats, as can be seen in this photograph. By this stage of the war most of the dark-blue trousers had worn out and been replaced by the lighter sky-blue material. Although regulations often stated that the men should wear regimental numbers, company letters, bugle horns and black ostrich feathers, many of them had lost these or had opted to only have some on their hats. The original orders that the hats were not to be turned up were also ignored: some had them turned on the left or the right and some not at all. Again, by this stage some of the men would have retained their leggings, while others would have acquired blanket rolls rather than knapsacks.

(**Below**) The Irish Brigade was known as 'the sons of Erin'. Thomas Francis Meagher, who wore a suit of dark-green velvet, trimmed with gold lace, led them. His men went into battle carrying a green regimental flag featuring an Irish harp under a fiery and cloudy sky. On their hats they had a brass Irish harp device. Their golden hour came at the battle of Antietam in September 1862, when the 63rd, 69th and 88th New York, together with the 29th Massachusetts, stormed the Confederate positions at great cost in an area that would become known as Bloody Lane.

Sharpshooters

DURING the Civil War there were two green-uniformed regiments in Union service: the 1st and 2nd US Sharpshooter Regiments. The noted engineer and marksman Hiram Berdan suggested that the best shots in the northern states be grouped together to form an elite unit of sharpshooters.

Washington adopted the idea and Berdan was given leave to form his own unit, specifying the weapons, uniform and equipment. A circular was sent out calling for applicants, the entry test requiring the men to put ten bullets in succession into a 10in (25cm) circle at 200yd (180m) with a rest, and from the shoulder at 100yd (90m).

The 1st Regiment was formed from men from New York, Michigan, Vermont, New Hampshire and Wisconsin, ten companies in all. The 2nd Regiment was drawn from men from New Hampshire, Vermont, Minnesota, Michigan, Pennsylvania and Maine, and never exceeded eight companies. The regiments underwent extensive training outside Washington from September 1861 to March 1862.

(**Right**) Berdan decided that the men would be issued with the breech-loading Sharps rifle. At the time the rifle cost $35, against $12 for a Springfield. Two companies of the 1st Regiment were equipped with target rifles, but these proved to be ineffective in early skirmishes. The uniforms were made of fine material, with a dark-green coat and cap (with a black plume) and, initially, light-blue trousers; these trousers were later replaced with dark-green items. The men were given leather leggings and hair-covered calfskin knapsacks from which they carried their cooking kits. A correspondent of the *New York Post* described them as looking like Robin Hood's outlaws.

(Opposite) The Berdan Sharpshooter uniform was made of the standard US Army wool; its colour was designed to allow the men to blend in with the foliage and trees during the leafy season. The forage cap usually sported a black ostrich feather. The men wore brogan shoes and brown leather gaiters that rose to the knee to protect the legs when walking through brush. The buttons of the uniform were made from hard, black rubber to eliminate light reflection. The men's leather accoutrements were a simple waist belt with cartridge box, cap box and bayonet. The knapsack was unique in the sense that it was a

Prussian design comprising a wooden frame covered with cowhide, hair-side out. A square mess kit was usually tied to the outside of the pack by leather straps.

(Above) The forage cap has a black leather McDowell peak. On the top of the cap are the corps, regimental and company insignia. The frock coat has nine buttons with a pale emerald-green piping. The enlisted men were issued with heavy, coarse, white or grey flannel shirts; these had a fold-down collar and were pulled over the head. The trousers were cut full and un-creased, with a button

fly and buttons on the high waist for braces (which were not issued). The boots were actually supplied as left and right boots and had a rough leather exterior. The gaiters were made from pigskin and buckled high to the knee; they were fastened with buckles up the leg and under the boot. The men tended to use the M1855 cartridge box as it was larger than the Sharps-pattern box.

(Below) Each of the men usually carried around forty rounds of ammunition in the cartridge box; an additional twenty were carried in the knapsack. If the sharpshooters were expected to be

engaged for a prolonged period of time, the issue would be increased to 100 rounds. Ideally, the men could fire up to ten aimed shots a minute. Officially the regiments constituted a brigade, but they were seldom deployed as such. In many cases, the companies were scattered and deployed as skirmishers. This meant that the men were often at the forefront of the battle lines, probing and always in contact with the enemy. Losses were inevitable and Berdan always ensured that sufficient replacements were being trained to replace his dead or seriously wounded men.

(Above) The Berdan Sharpshooters' first action came on 27 September 1861 when C and E companies of the 1st Regiment engaged a group of Confederate foragers at Lewinsville, Virginia. The Sharpshooters were to feature in at least sixty-five actions; notably, they were present at South Mountain, Chancellorsville and Gettysburg. The men received their full issue of Sharps rifles in May 1862. The rifles were open-sighted and shot a .52-calibre ball. The men used Lawrence Pellet primers rather than the standard 'hat' percussion caps. The Sharps rifle, being a breech-loader, allowed the men to load and fire from the prone position. The men tended to use an angular bayonet rather than the sword bayonet.

(Below) A Berdan's sharpshooter using a cartridge-model Sharps rifle with a long, brass, tube telescopic sight. Most of the men in Company E of the 2nd Regiment were issued a bayonet-fitted, double-set trigger, Model 1859 Sharps .52-calibre breech-loading rifle; some in the company were armed with heavy, telescopic target rifles. Often patrolling from the front line, it was their responsibility to discover the enemy's deployment. With the enemy located, the Sharpshooters shifted back to reinforce the infantry. Usually positioned at a flank, they delivered long-range fire, targeting officers, artillery batteries and enemy snipers. There were approximately 2,570 Union snipers during the Civil War. Of this total 1,008 were killed or wounded, giving them a casualty rate of 40 per cent even though they never charged or closed with the enemy. Although records indicate that thousands of their unique uniform coats were issued and worn by these two distinguished regiments, only a single known specimen – housed in the Smithsonian Institution – has survived to modern times.

Union Cavalry

ON the eve of the American Civil War the United States Army had just five regiments of mounted troops: the 1st and 2nd Dragoons, the 1st and 2nd Cavalry and the Mounted Rifles. These units were arrayed on the western extremities of the nation – there was not a single cavalry unit within 1,000 miles of Washington.

When war came in 1861, the cavalry had no experience of involvement in major operations, let alone the combined operations that would be required of them in the war. Also, many cavalry officers resigned and joined the Confederates, including four of the regimental colonels and seventeen of the twenty officers in the 2nd Cavalry.

The cavalry's primary role was to support the infantry and artillery. They were also required to gather intelligence, to scout and to screen the movements of the army. This was, at least, the theory during the early months of the war: increasingly, as the conflict developed, they were used as an offensive arm of the Union Army.

In 1861, the US Army reorganized its mounted forces. The old 1st Dragoons became the 1st US Cavalry, and the 2nd Dragoons the 2nd US Cavalry. The Mounted Rifles were transformed into the 3rd and confusingly, the old 1st Cavalry became the 4th and the 2nd became the 5th. In the summer of 1861 a new regiment was created, the only new regular regiment created during the war; this was the 6th Cavalry with its men enlisting for five years instead of the usual three.

To begin with the commander of the Army of the Potomac, Major General George B. McClellan, did not wish to place any trust in the cavalry. He believed that it would take at least five years before they could become a credible fighting force. As a result, the new volunteer regiments were broken up, many companies being assigned to infantry brigades to act as glorified messengers.

The regular cavalry were brigaded as a Cavalry Reserve Brigade. Although the 5th were deployed at the Battle of Gaines Mill during the battle of the Seven Days in June 1862, McClellan used the remainder of the cavalry ineffectually. In early June 1862, the cavalry were led by Colonel Phillip St George Cooke against his son-in-law J.E.B. Stuart's Confederate horsemen. Stuart was a consummate leader: Cooke was outmanoeuvred and ultimately replaced.

In June 1862 Major General John Pope took command of the newly raised Army of Virginia: McClellan would operate in the Shenandoah Valley and central Virginia while Pope operated on the Virginia Peninsula. Pope only had volunteer cavalry brigades, but these performed well for him under Brigadier Generals George D. Bayard and John Buford. Pope's army was decisively defeated at the Second Manassas in August 1862 and he was replaced; what remained of his forces became part of the Army of the Potomac in the first week of September 1862.

At the Battle of Antietam, the Union cavalry were barely used: what was in fact the bloodiest battle of the war saw only twelve cavalry casualties. One brigade of cavalry was involved, safety tucked away behind the artillery batteries, and it came to very little harm, though a cannonball decapitated its commander. Buford was in overall command of the cavalry with Brigadier General Alfred Pleasonton commanding the troops in the field. McClellan repeatedly refused to commit or trust his cavalry, and

(Right) The mounted figure in the centre is a musician, distinguished by the stripes and frame of coloured braid in yellow on his chest. The musician would carry a regulation issue bugle with a yellow branch-of-service cord and tassels. Mounted officers, such as the figure on the left, were issued with regulation frock coats; this officer lacks his branch-of-service shoulder straps. He wears a narrow, peaked cap, very popular with the cavalry officers. He carries an officer's sabre and wears a sash around his waist. The cavalry sergeant wears a dress jacket without his shoulder scales. The sergeant's cap has his branch-of-service badge; around his waist would be a cap box, holster, pistol-cartridge box and carbine-cartridge box.

as a result the Confederate cavalry had the run of the field and caused immense damage to his army. In November 1862, McClellan was replaced by Major General Ambrose E. Burnside. He, too, had no idea how to use the cavalry, and in the attacks on Fredericksburg in December the cavalry only lost three men, one of whom was Bayard.

Major General Joseph Hooker replaced Burnside in January 1863; he set about reorganizing the Army of the Potomac and created a cavalry corps of some 12,000 men. Major General George Stoneman was in overall command while Pleasonton, Gregg and Averell took command of a division each, with Buford in command of the Reserve Brigade. The Union cavalry would not have to wait long before their first victory. It came on 17 March 1863 when Buford and Averell defeated Confederate Brigadier General Fitzhugh Lee at Kelly's Ford.

Stoneman's corps was sent on a deep raid into Confederate territory just prior to the Battle of Chancellorsville, the intention being to cut off Lee's communications with Richmond. Hooker was decisively defeated at Chancellorsville and he blamed Stoneman and Averell; both were relieved of their commands. Pleasonton took over as corps commander, Buford took command of the 1st Division and Colonel Alfred Duffy assumed leadership of the 3rd Division.

The Battle of Brandy Station was fought on 9 June 1863 against J.E.B. Stuart's cavalry. In this, the largest cavalry battle of the war a total of some 21,000 Union and Confederate cavalry were engaged. This all-mounted battle spilled over two days, the Confederates slowly gaining the upper hand. The two sides were not done with one another, however: they clashed again at Aldie, Middleburg and Upperville, deep into Pennsylvania.

These battles were the opening clashes of the Gettysburg Campaign. Buford denied the Confederates the chance to take Gettysburg and held his position until reinforced by the infantry. The Union cavalry had finally proved that they could match the skills of the Confederate horsemen and their actions, commanders and enlisted men would form the backbone of the post-war US Cavalry.

(Below) A union cavalry trooper would have been issued with a hat and a forage cap. In essence these were identical to those issued to the infantry, and dated back to around 1858. This troop of cavalry wear the forage cap. At least in theory, all of the men would have had both hats issued throughout the war, but many preferred the forage cap. The hat was a model 1858 type; many of these were made in New York and at least 50,000 of these were ordered and subsequently delivered from 1861. The hat tended to be looped up on the right side and held there with a brass eagle device. The cavalryman would also have his crossed sabre badge and the regimental number on the front of the crown. As additional ornamentation on the hat, the men would have a yellow wool cord with tassels, and a black feather attached in front lying to the opposite side from the looped side of the hat.

(Right) This Union cavalry officer would have been issued with a regulation frock coat. However, like many of the non-commissioned officers and enlisted men, he has opted to wear a dress jacket with shoulder scales. This short, plain jacket had either one or two rows of buttons, according to his grade.

(Left) In addition to ensuring that his own equipment was kept in serviceable order, a cavalryman was also responsible for ensuring that his horse and its equipment were regularly maintained. The picture depicts a typical bridle and bit arrangement for Union cavalry during the Civil War. Horses needed to be responsive to their riders, who would often have to manoeuvre their mounts while firing and loading a carbine, often in difficult terrain. In the majority of cases a cavalry unit would deploy up to two-thirds of its strength as skirmishers, effectively as mounted infantry. A section would be retained as horse holders and to prevent the mounts from bolting when the firing began.

(Below) This cavalry bugler has his branch-of-service colour braid on his chest. He is sounding an issue bugle, again with branch-of-service cord and tassels. The sergeant accompanying him shows that he is a first sergeant by three stripes and a lozenge on his arm. Note that the men are equipped for an extended period away from camp, as they have their personal equipment and blanket rolls attached to their saddles.

(Right) This picture represents a man from H Company of the 4th Michigan Volunteer Cavalry, who were in existence between 1862 and 1865. The regiment saw considerable service in Kentucky, Tennessee, Georgia and Alabama, and was involved in the pursuit and capture of the Confederate President Jefferson Davis, who was captured at Irwinsville, Georgia, on 10 May 1865. The individual in this picture has the familiar crossed-sabres design between his regimental number and company letter.

(**Opposite**) This Union cavalry first sergeant would have been issued with the standard kit consisting of cap, blouse, dress jacket, a single pair of reinforced trousers, two flannel shirts, two pairs of drawers (underpants), two pairs of stockings, a pair of boots, an overcoat, a blanket, a knapsack and a canteen with straps. This sergeant wears gauntlets: these were not issued to the troopers but they were particularly useful for riding, and heavy buff leather gloves with gauntlet cuffs were the most popular, as can be seen in this example.

(**Below**) Another shot of the cavalry sergeant; this time we see the back detail of his short, dark-blue jacket, which is trimmed with yellow braid. This is essentially a fatigue tunic, also known as a blouse. It reached to just below the hip bone, and had four buttons to the front and an inside left-breast pocket. Officers were permitted to wear waist-length jackets, as frock coats were impracticable on horseback.

(Above) This cavalry standard-bearer has the double-breasted winter overcoat, with a stand-up collar and cape, which almost reaches the cuffs. Sky-blue overcoats and capes were predominantly issued, although some of the men obtained dark-blue issues. Non-commissioned officers had their chevrons on the lower sleeves of the overcoat so that their rank was still visible when the cape was being worn. By and large, officers were issued with dark-blue overcoats, but in the later years of the war they were granted permission to wear enlisted men's overcoats in order to make them less obvious targets for snipers.

(Opposite) Here we see a Union cavalryman wearing laced booties; these were a higher-ankle version of the infantryman's brogan shoes. In practice many of the men bought boots of their own, tending to favour calf-length or higher boots and often opting for ones with flaps covering their knees. The men would purchase these themselves or have them sent from home.

(Left) Until December 1861 the cavalry were issued with dark-blue trousers. After this date they wore the familiar light sky-blue that Washington had discovered was cheaper to manufacture. The trousers were reinforced with a double thickness of cloth on the inside of the legs, which to some extent prolonged the durability of the garment. The jackets and trousers were all made of wool, which made them uncomfortable in the summer months.

(**Below**) The trooper's saddle equipment was the 1859 McClellan model, which had been adapted from European models. The troopers were issued with saddle equipment including saddlebags, a picket pin, a feedbag, a rope and a leather boot on which to rest the carbine. The other two major items were the cavalryman's sword-belt and carbine sling. On his belt he would have a holster for his revolver, a cartridge box, a cap box and his sabre in a scabbard.

(**Opposite**) The bulk of the leather equipment was provided in saddle-grade, buff-brown or black leather – both versions turned black after a short period of time. The men generally wore the revolver holster over the right hip, with the butt of the pistol facing to the front. This proved to be the most effective way of carrying the weapon as it could be cross-drawn with the left hand. Interestingly, most of the cavalrymen were trained to shoot with their left hand as they used their right hand to control the horse.

(Left) Attached to the rear-left of the belt was a shoulder strap. This was a narrow strap with a hook on the end that was placed over the right shoulder, then hooked onto a ring sewn onto the left of the front of the belt; it could also be secured with a buckle. It was designed to assist the holding up of the belt once the heavy sabre had been attached, though many of the troopers cut the straps off and discarded them.

(Below) The cavalryman's holster was secured by a flap that fitted onto a stub sewn on the front. The sabre scabbard had two rings attached to it, which in turn were attached to the belt either by two leather straps that hung from the belt or by two brass closures. The straps were of different lengths, the one at the front closest to the belt-buckle being shorter: the idea was that the sword would hang with its grip towards the trooper. He could take the sword out with his left hand and maintain control of the horse with his right.

(Opposite) These cavalrymen clearly show their cap- and cartridge boxes attached to their belts. Normally the cartridge box was worn on the right-rear of the belt so that the trooper could easily reach backwards for it with his right hand. The leather box had a flap that could be fixed with a stud and inside there was a wooden or metal box for the carbine cartridges. Troopers would also wear a smaller cartridge belt that contained cartridges for the revolver. The cap box was a small, round, leather box in which there was a tin box of percussion caps and, in most cases, loose caps that could be used for both the carbine and the revolver. Sheepskin was sewn into the cap box to prevent the caps from bouncing out, especially when riding at high speed.

(**Opposite**) Here we see Union cavalry equipment, including the sabre and belt. The brass buckles and belt-plates tended to be square with a spread-eagle surrounded by a silver wreath. Many of the cavalry units, particularly if they were volunteer cavalry, wore their own state belt-buckle or some other unique design.

(**Below**) This first sergeant provides a good view of the carbine that was the trooper's main weapon. Cavalrymen tended to wear a wide leather sling with a strap attached; the carbine was then secured to the strap by a ring. The sling was usually worn over the left shoulder, often under the belt sling. The carbine sling had a large brass buckle on the chest and often troopers secured their carbine cartridge box to this sling instead of to the belt. In this case the sergeant has attached his carbine to his saddle.

(Below) In July 1864 the 2nd Iowa Cavalry were wearing so many non-issue garments that they were ordered to burn them. Many of the troopers purchased hats, coats and trousers, and even civilian clothing and Confederate garments and equipment. The men found that civilian clothing and hats, in particular, were far more comfortable and more durable than issue items. Many of the men, particularly in hot weather, wore cotton or denim rather than regulation wool clothing.

(Opposite top) This picture shows the 1859 McClellan military saddle. The saddle has an open, metal-reinforced wooden tree. The saddle skirts are of harness leather and are screwed to the sidebars. The stirrups were usually made of hickory or wood. The saddle had a durable, rawhide-covered tree and in 1861 brass hardware replaced the iron. The saddle included a small saddlebag, a nosebag, picket pin, lariat and cone. It also had a boot on the right side of the saddle that could hold the carbine.

(Opposite below) At the beginning of the war the Union cavalry was given full-dress headgear: a stiff, broad-brimmed hat that was turned up on one side. These were quickly discarded and replaced by the forage cap or kepi. Theoretically an enlisted man was supposed to show only his regimental number on his kepi, but for the most part the men ignored this and attached the cross-sabre brass badge that was the insignia of the cavalry corps.

(**Opposite top**) Large flags would have been unmanageable on horseback, so these swallow-tailed flags – known as guidons – were just over 2–2½ ft (60–90cm) square. Initially they were two-colour red over white, but after 1862 the familiar red and white stripes and the blue canton were introduced to match the national colours. Most of the stars were arranged in two concentric rings with the company letter painted in the centre.

(**Opposite below**) Cavalry standards and guidons were flown from 9ft (2.7m) staffs. They had a brass spear-point and a brass butt-cap. The colour bearers had a small leather cup or boot beside their stirrup leathers in which to place the butt of the staff. In effect these were scaled-down versions of the national colours; some of them had the regimental number, but others were just plain and not necessarily swallow-tailed.

(**Above**) This cavalry flag is a post-January 1862 model that shows the troop letter within the stars area. There was no pattern set for the placement of the stars on the flag and consequently they could appear in circles, ovals or rows. The manufacturers of the flags merely interpreted the regulations – some added mottoes, coats of arms, eagles or other designs.

(Left) The bulk of the cavalry was ultimately armed with the Model 1860 sabre. This was their close-quarters weapon, primarily used in charges and pursuits. It was a fearsome weapon when swung from a galloping horse, capable of severing limbs and even, in extreme cases, of decapitation. This trooper carries his sabre ceremonially over his right shoulder, while maintaining control of the reins with his left hand.

(Above) Philip St George Cooke was considered to be the father of the US Cavalry. He had considerable experience as an officer, having graduated from West Point in 1827. His views on cavalry tactics influenced the role of the cavalry early in the war, despite the fact that many army commanders had little or no interest or experience in the deployment of cavalry.

(Right) The cavalryman would use a Colt Model 1860 .44 armoured pistol. This was fitted to his waist belt with the butt of the pistol facing forward so that he could retrieve the piece easily with his left hand. The pistols were used for close-quarter fighting when it was impracticable to use the carbine. In many cases the sabre and pistol were used in conjunction with one another for maximum effect prior to collision with an enemy unit.

(Opposite) The US Cavalry was armed with a huge array of different carbine models. Initially, the regular cavalry was issued with an M1855 muzzle-loading .58-calibre pistol-carbine, with a larger hand stock and shorter barrel than the M1855 rifled musket. The most popular carbine was the Spencer breech-loader, seen here, which was just like the Spencer infantry rifle; the Union Army acquired 110,500 of these carbines by the end of the war. The Spencer carbine gave an enormous rate of fire, which meant that small cavalry detachments could hold up far larger enemy formations.

(Above) Here we can see the back detail of the Union cavalry jackets. The men have drawn their sabres and are ready to charge. The men have sheathed their carbines. Many of them were issued with M1859 or M1863 Sharp's breech-loaders, and the Union Army purchased around 50,000 of these. Others were armed with the Burnside breech-loader, which had a brass cartridge and a separate percussion cap. Four different models of this type were made, amounting to 55,000 weapons.

(**Opposite top**) These two cavalrymen have dispensed with their firearms and have resorted to a full charge using their sabres. In reality cavalry charges were rare and the cavalry would only be committed to such a charge after the main resistance of an enemy formation had already been broken, either by artillery or by sustained musket and carbine fire.

(**Opposite below**) Here a charging cavalry unit faces the long-range peril of artillery ball and shell. Clearly the casualties that could be caused to this large, if fast-moving, target would have been considerable. They would be engaged by artillery fire at extreme distance. The artillery would revert to shell and then to canister, by which time the cavalry would be within effective musket range. The days of cavalry breaking formed infantry regiments had long since passed, and due to the firepower of the infantry regiments there was no pressing need for them to do as their Napoleonic predecessors had done and form a square.

(**Below**) The foremost figure in this group of charging cavalry holds his carbine in his right hand. Many of the cavalry were also issued with Smith carbines, of which over 30,000 were purchased. They were not liked, however, as dirt around the breech tended to cause burns on the firer's face. A huge number of other carbines was produced by private manufacturers, including the Gallagher Starr, Maynard, Remington, Merrill, Joslyn, Cosmopolitan, Warner, Ballard, Gibbs, Ball, Palmer, Lindner and Wesson.

Union Artillery

WHEN war broke out between the states in 1861, the artillery component of the army was undoubtedly the smallest. It remained the smallest branch throughout the war and reached a maximum of 12 per cent of the total strength of the Union Army, with some 432 batteries.

Field artillery was commonly referred to as light artillery and, broadly, can be split into two distinct types: mounted artillery, only the drivers and officers of which were mounted; and horse artillery, in which all of the men were horsed. Again generally, the mounted artillery accompanied the infantry and horse artillery accompanied the cavalry.

Usually a battery had either six or four guns, although some batteries might have eight. A captain commanded each battery and each section (a pair of guns) was commanded by a lieutenant. The section often operated to all intents and purposes as an independent unit for small-scale actions. Each of the guns was under the command of a sergeant with two corporals, one the gunner and the other responsible for the 'caisson' in which the ammunition and powder was carried. Seven or eight men directly served the gun, but twenty-five to thirty men were necessary to keep a single gun in the field and in operating condition.

The distinguishing colour for the artillery was red. The enlisted men sometimes wore the sack coat, but more commonly they wore a waist-length shell jacket that was trimmed with red worsted tape. Kepis and forage caps had a red band around the base, or were entirely of red cloth. Non-commissioned officers' chevrons and trouser stripes were also red, as was the background of the officers' shoulder straps.

The enlisted men were issued crossed cannons in stamped brass to mount on their hats. In addition, they had a brass number designating the artillery regiment and a letter designating their battery. Officers tended to wear an embroidered version of the design.

On the battlefield an artillery flag marked the position of the battery. State units tended to use a guidon that was essentially a small version of the Stars and Stripes with a forked tail. Regular Union artillery units preferred the larger rectangular yellow flags with crossed cannons.

Prior to the war, the army mostly used 6- and 12-pounder field guns, 12-, 24- and 32-pounder field howitzers, 18- and 24-pounder siege and garrison guns, and 32- and 42-pounder coast guns. The great need for ordnance during the war meant that the Union Army began to acquire a multitude of different weapons from aboard, notably Armstrongs, Blakelys, Wiards and Whitworths; the Parrott rifles are the most recognizable with their reinforcing band of wrought iron. Captain Robert Parker Parrott invented the Parrott rifle and it became one of the most common types of rifled piece used by the Union Army.

The principles of rifling had been understood long before the Civil War. The spin of the projectile caused by the spiral grooves in the barrel made it fly further and straighter, and hit the target with greater power. A number of older weapons, particularly the obsolete 6-pounders, were re-bored with rifling, but they were of limited use. But the cast iron proved to be too brittle so Parrott, who developed a system by which the reinforcing band was clamped in place while the barrel was rotated, used superior smelting techniques. This meant that the iron band was uniformly attached to the barrel and barrel bursts were far more rare.

Parrott's system reduced the price of a rifled piece from $350 to $187. The rifled piece, which became known as the Parrott, was to become the workhouse of the artillery and was preferred by the artillery crews even after the introduction of the ordnance rifle, a hammer-welded, iron, rifled artillery piece that became the second most common rifle field artillery piece. Steel rifles eventually superseded the Parrott, the first semi-steel variety being the Wiard. Smaller rifles, such as Whitworths and Armstrongs, were made of true steel.

(Opposite top) It was usual for six horses, in pairs, to pull artillery pieces in the field. An artilleryman would ride on each left horse of the pair – this was vital to ensure that the horses were under constant control and that they could be quickly manoeuvred into position. Here we see a pair of horses pulling a caisson with the artillerymen walking alongside. The 'driver' of the pair of horses would use a short whip or stick to either tap or lash the horses when necessary. Horse artillery allowed all of the crew to be mounted for swift movement onto and off the battlefield while, as we see here, foot artillery only allowed for a proportion of the crew to ride on the horses or on the caisson (some also rode on the ammunition chest).

(Opposite below) In this second shot of an artillery limber and crew, the remainder of the crew shepherd along a 'Napoleon' artillery piece (so called because it was a Napoleonic-era design). Note the white, long-length gauntlets to protect the hands in cases when the limber or gun became stuck in mud or ruts. In this example, the crew only appear to have side arms (revolvers), instead of the issue sabre for close protection. Some have the familiar shorter jacket, while the man in the foreground nearest the caisson has a longer jacket. Both types were issued to the men at various stages of the war. The vast majority of the men, ultimately, came to wear the forage cap or kepi. Many volunteers who believed that they had been posted to an infantry regiment discovered that the entire unit was impressed to become an artillery regiment; they would be posted in this role to defend garrisons and vital points around Washington.

(**Left**) Regulations stated that non-commissioned officers should wear a red stripe on their trousers. In this case, both the sergeant and the artilleryman wear boots: these were issued to most artillerymen, while others were issued with the standard black brogues as issued to the infantrymen. The usual course of events was that the mounted components of the artillery unit were issued with boots in the same way as the cavalry while the foot-based artillerymen were issued with shoes in line with other foot troops. Both men wear the M1858 forage cap, indicating a period later than 1861. In the first year of war the artillery was issued with a hat similar to a shako, with a hard body and a wide and stiff visor. It quickly proved to be wholly unsuitable for the rigours of the battlefield.

(Right) Dating back to 1836, the prescribed insignia for the artillery was a pair of crossed cannon, which device is just visible on the cap of this artillery sergeant. Although the crossed cannon are the dominant feature on the cap, it also featured the battery (company) letter; unassigned independent batteries would only feature the number of the battery. Heavy artillery regiments would have the crossed cannons, the regimental number and the battery letter. Usually, these three devices were worn on the army dress hat rather than the forage cap; the dress hat also featured a red tassel and cord, a black ostrich feather and a brass eagle. If the heavy artillery were just wearing the forage cap, then all of the brass insignia, apart from the eagle, would be worn on the top of the cap.

(Opposite top) Light artillerymen, such as these soldiers, whether volunteers or regulars, were issued with both the fatigue blouse and the waist-length jacket. The jacket has a standard identifying scarlet trim, a twelve-button front and a standing collar. The artilleryman with gauntlets in the foreground wears his fatigue blouse under his jacket; this was a four-button garment identical in style and issue to the blouse distributed to the infantry. The men were issued with two different types of trousers. Both of the sets were made of sky-blue kersey material. The standard pair was identical to those issued to the infantry and tended to be issued to the artillery crew. The other type was issued to those who were mounted on the horse teams and had an additional layer of material to protect against wear from the saddle.

(**Left**) This artillery corporal carries a model 1840 light-artillery sabre in a scabbard from his waist belt. Just visible is his holster containing a Colt Model 1860 army revolver. He wears the M1858 forage cap, the most common headgear for the artillery. By November 1863 the general rule was for artillerymen to be instructed to wear the regulation forage cap to the exclusion of all other types of cap. The order did not prohibit non-commissioned officers from wearing other caps of better construction and material, provided they were of a broadly similar appearance to the forage cap. Many of the non-commissioned officers, in particular, chose to have their jackets altered to give a more tailored appearance; they also tended to have the collar slightly lowered. Jacket alterations cost a little more than 50 cents.

(**Opposite right**) The routine of firing an artillery piece varied little unless it was a specialized cannon. Number 2 Gunner was handed a cartridge (ball and powder), which he placed in the muzzle of the gun. Number 1 Gunner rammed the cartridge down the barrel all the way to the bottom. Meanwhile, Number 3 Gunner held his thumb over the vent in the breech. Once the cartridge was in place, he jabbed a hole in the cloth bag at the base of the cartridge to expose the black powder. Number 4 Gunner then placed a friction primer into the vent and attached a lanyard to the primer. The men then stood back and Number 4 Gunner pulled the lanyard to fire the piece. The process would be repeated, preceded by Number 1 Gunner ramming a wet sponge down the barrel to extinguish any residual embers.

(**Right**) Shoulder scales had become universal in the pre-war army, worn in the same way as cloth epaulettes. Scales made of brass were issued to volunteers, and some light-artillery batteries wore them, although this was the exception rather than the rule. Shoulder scales tended to only be worn on parades, when the artillerymen were also expected to wear their jackets. Officers wore a Russian-style shoulder knot, battery officers wearing up to three rows of braid, dependent upon their rank. The crew here is seen with their full equipment ready for firing including the ramrod propped up against the cannon. Personal weapons are not visible in the picture, but the men would have been issued with a sabre and/or a revolver, rather than the unpopular Model 1833 foot-artillery short sword.

Union Camp Life

LIFE in an army camp, whether during training, on garrison duty or in the field, was a tedious and repetitive round of duties, drilling and the constant search for any form of entertainment. For many of the men this was their first period of time away from home. It quickly made the men hard and self-sufficient. Swearing was frowned upon and officers would fine men as much as a day's pay if one of their oaths reached the officer's ears. Gambling was commonplace, including poker, dice-rolling games and any other means by which they could bet, including fist fights. Fighting was in fact commonplace, particularly if rival regiments were placed anywhere near one another in the camp. Fights routinely broke out between Germans, Irishmen or African-Americans. The men drank whiskey and many of them tried to ferment anything that they could find to produce alcohol.

(**Below**) A cavalry troop passes through a heavily used track in a Union camp. Note the tent to the rear, near the tree line: this would have been used as an impromptu officers' mess. Constant cavalry patrols would be mounted in order to protect the camp and warn of enemy movements in the area. Note also the Stars and Stripes, overlaid with the number 2, denoting the rallying point for the camp.

(**Opposite**) An infantryman sits beside a fire in camp, having chopped and prepared the wood for the cooking. Soldiers would spend as much time as was necessary foraging, which actually meant stealing from the local population or from other units if their food or equipment was not protected. Billy Crump, of the 23rd Ohio Infantry, stole the future nineteenth President's horse, the then Colonel Rutherford B. Hayes. He looted for two days in West Virginia and brought back with him fifty chickens, twenty dozen eggs and 30lb (14kg) of butter, in addition to the horse.

(Right) This image represents the Federal colours, with a dark blue field, gold tassel and braiding. The regimental flag would be displayed beside the tenting area of the regiment, and would invariably be protected by a colour guard.

(Opposite) Some 300,000 men from Ohio enlisted in the Union Army, raising 200 infantry regiments. Some 35,500 men were killed from this state alone during the war. This is a first sergeant of the 8th Ohio. The original strength of this regiment had been forty-five officers and 944 enlisted men. They saw action in every campaign of the Army of the Potomac from Antietam to Petersburg – when they mustered out towards the end of the war the numbers present were 168 men.

(Left) Union and Confederate soldiers often traded in scarcities with one another. Union infantry wanted Virginia tobacco, while the Rebels were always short of coffee. Here we see a typical wrought-iron camp fire, which would be kept alight throughout the duration of the men's stay in that area. The tents in the background are typical A-frame issue of white cotton, which were designed for easy erection and dismantling.

(Opposite) This infantryman wears long johns under his uniform. The Union Army issued 10.7 million pairs of flannel drawers to their men. The men preferred long johns, and the drawers were rarely worn. Officially the drawers were tan and around two-thirds of the leg length, with buttons on the waistband and fly.

(Right) Despite having to carry additional equipment, men who could play musical instruments were in great demand. This banjo player is seen with a cotton shirt. The cuffs were made by simply turning back the sleeves and then sewing them down; they tended not to have pockets. Originally the men were issued with grey shirts and the Union Army purchased over 11 million of these, in addition to nearly 14,000,000yd (13,000,000m) of grey cloth or cotton to make more shirts.

(**Opposite top**) This infantry officer wears a Hardee hat with embroidered badges. An embroidered gold crescent surrounds his regimental number on the front of the hat and he has ornate black and gold tassels around the crown. Clearly visible is his waistcoat underneath the jacket, which has three plain, pressed-brass buttons on each cuff.

(**Below**) An array of A-frame infantry tents. They were a standard 6ft (1.8m) high at the ridge and around 8ft 9in (2.7m) wide at the base, and ideally suited for two men. The tents would usually have been carried by a wagon or a group of wagons attached to each regiment or brigade when the camp was moved on.

(**Opposite below**) Those men that could read carried with them books and newspapers, which they read avidly regardless of their age or condition. Here an infantryman, alongside a corporal, reads a copy of *Harper's Weekly*. The weekly newspaper was already established before the Civil War and provided for many of the men their only source of information regarding the progress of the war.

(**Opposite**) This campfire scene features United States Colored Infantry and white non-commissioned officers and officers. In practice it was unlikely that the men would mix socially. Here the troops are seen in woodland prior to battle. Note the lack of insignia and distinguishing signs on the uniforms, with the exception of the crouched man next to the first sergeant, who appears to have a corps badge with F Company, 20th Regiment over the Jäger bugle on his kepi.

(**Right**) This infantry sergeant wears a standard fatigue jacket and an unadorned Union kepi. Under his jacket he wears a civilian blue and white checked shirt. Non-commissioned officers took the bulk of the responsibility for camp discipline and were required to ensure that the men were allocated sufficient duties to keep them as much out of mischief as possible. Officers tended to attend only parades, religious ceremonies and briefings to the men prior to engagement in battle.

(**Below**) This mixed group of infantry display the full range of different jackets, including the frock, sack and fatigue coat. The individual in the centre has a light blue-grey overcoat and cape. Visible next to the standard-bearer is a member of the US Sharpshooters. Note also the difference in colour of the trousers, ranging from grey to sky blue and then to dark blue. The men also display different hats: two wear the Hardee hat, while the rest wear kepis.

(Opposite top) Vivandieres were dressed to all intents and purposes like Zouaves, except that they had voluminous red skirts instead of trousers. Vivandieres were dubbed 'daughters of the regiment' and frequently marched into battle with their male counterparts. The women were uniformed to establish their rank and position, and they often provided morale-boosting comfort and encouragement for the men.

(Opposite below) Even the smallest and sharpest of actions would create inevitable casualties and produce a clutch of prisoners. Here we see a company of Union infantry returning to camp with their dead and wounded, one of whom is supported by two captured Confederate infantrymen. Note that even for scouting and raiding purposes the men leave camp fully accoutred. In this winter scene at least three of the men have gaiters over their shoes in order to protect their footwear from the wet and mud.

(Above) This group represents the 69th New York Infantry Regiment. Note the use of green as facings to denote that they are an Irish regiment. This group illustrates the general standardization of uniform, even for the drummer boys at the front of the group. Camp followers, probably wives of the unit, have accompanied them on campaign.

(Right) Female camp followers, including cooks and seamstresses, would accompany the regiment either on an official or on an unofficial basis. Many of the men would crave for the comfort of home cooking, which to some extent could be provided by these women. Here we see a civilian woman with a head shawl tied around the neck with a bow.

(Opposite) Many of the battles inflicted huge casualties in terms of dead, wounded and missing on the Union Army. Their bloodiest battles were: Chancellorsville in May 1862, where they lost 17,000 (16 per cent of those engaged); Spotsylvania in May 1864 when 18,500 (20 per cent) were lost; and Gettysburg in July 1863 with 23,000 casualties, amounting to 27 per cent of their fighting strength. The army stood to lose at least 10 per cent and up to 30 per cent of its strength, whether it won or lost a battle. Here we see a medical orderly sergeant trying to staunch the wounds of a man with a head wound.

(Below) In addition to the US Army surgeons and doctors at hand, local doctors, if they had not already been impressed into the army, hastened to the battlefields to assist the wounded. Here we see a wounded infantryman being tended by such a civilian doctor. Note that he still wears his knapsack and bedroll, which he would be loathe to lose.

(Opposite) Officially medical officers, such as this surgeon, were considered to be a part of the headquarters' staff. Army regulations stated that when not working the surgeons would wear a medium or emerald green sash. They were also issued with an M1840 sword: this was not really designed for combat, as it was only 28in (70cm) long and ¾in (2cm) wide at the hilt.

(Below) Two medical orderlies attend to a wounded Union man. In practice, many of the orderlies were non-combatants attached to the regiments, such as musicians or members of the quartermaster's department. Their role was to quickly assess which men could be saved and then hand them over for treatment. Light wounds would be dealt with immediately, while more severe injuries could well mean that the infantryman was left there to die.

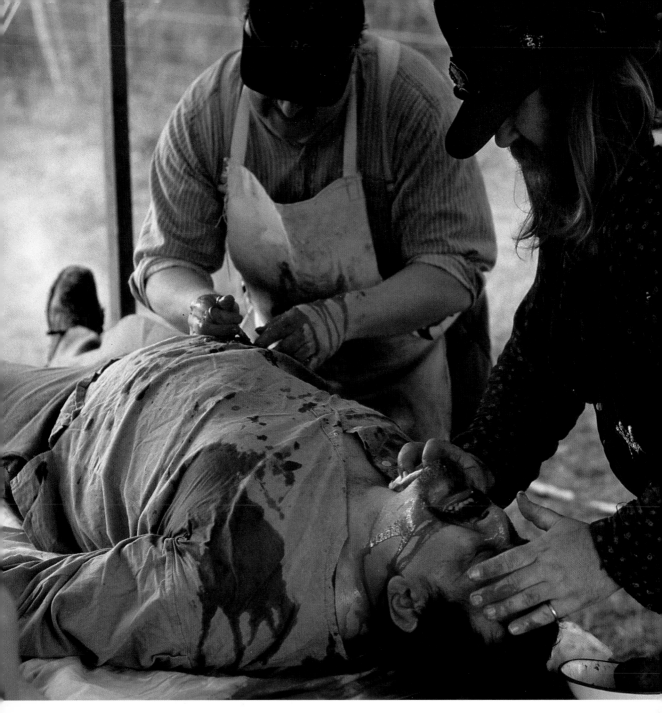

(Above) The army surgeons wore frocked coats with embroidered shoulder straps bearing two gold leaves and 'MS' embroidered in silver against a black background, standing for Medical Staff. The medical staff did their utmost to try to save the lives of grievously injured men, but the small-arms projectiles used in the war shattered bones beyond repair, added to which there was the ever-present danger of disease and infection.

Acknowledgements

The authors are indebted to the American Civil War Society and the innumerable photographers who provided these posed shots from a variety of public and private events during several re-enactment campaign seasons. Photographs are drawn from events at Cornbury Park, Weston Park and Steam, Strife and Secession. Individual photographers include Geoff Buxton, Ian Dunning of the Defence School of Photography and Mike McCormac. Thanks also go to the countless numbers of ACWS members for agreeing to be featured in this book.